Starting a Photography Business with Your Nikon D7000

How to Start a Freelance Photography Photo Business with the Nikon D7000 Camera

By Brian Mahoney

Join Our VIP Mailing List And Get FREE Money Making Training Videos! Then Start Making Money Within 24 Hours!
Plus If You Join Our Mailing List You Can Get Revised And New Edition Versions Of Your Book Free!

And Notifications of other FREE Offers!

Just Hit/Type in the Link Below

https://mahoneyproducts.wixsite.com/win1

Get Our Video Training Program at:

Zero Cost

Million Dollar

Internet Marketing

142 video series

Amazing Training Videos!

* YouTube Video Marketing

* Email Marketing

* Expert Copy writing

* Set up a Squeeze page

* Getting Massive Web Traffic

https://goo.gl/7t4XHY

ABOUT THE AUTHOR

Brian Mahoney is the author of over 250 business start-up books, real estate investing programs and Christian literature and software. He started his company MahoneyProducts in 1992.

For over two decades he has been a local and national speaker. He served overseas 2 tours in the United States Army and worked over a decade for the US Postal Service.

He has a degree in Information Technology from Henry Ford College in Dearborn Michigan.

He owns and runs 7 online businesses.

His books and video training programs have helped thousands of people all over the world start their own successful business.

http://www.briansmahoney.com/

DEDICATION

**This book is dedicated to my brother
Ulester Love Mahoney Jr.
A blessing from God and kind loving Man.**

ACKNOWLEDGMENTS

I WOULD LIKE TO ACKNOWLEDGE ALL THE HARD WORK OF THE MEN AND WOMEN OF THE UNITED STATES MILITARY, WHO RISK THEIR LIVES ON A DAILY BASIS, TO MAKE THE WORLD A SAFER PLACE.

Disclaimer

This book was written as a guide to starting a business. As with any other high yielding action, starting a business has a certain degree of risk. This book is not meant to take the place of accounting, legal, financial or other professional advice. If advice is needed in any of these fields, you are advised to seek the services of a professional.

While the author has attempted to make the information in this book as accurate as possible, no guarantee is given as to the accuracy or currency of any individual item. Laws and procedures related to business are constantly changing.

Therefore, in no event shall Brian Mahoney, the author of this book be liable for any special, indirect, or consequential damages or any damages whatsoever in connection with the use of the information herein provided.

Table of Contents

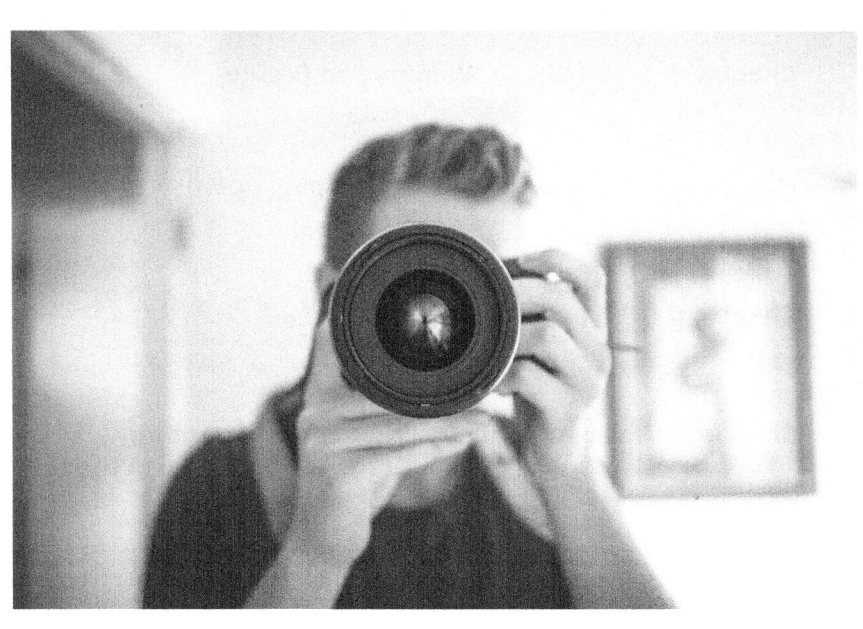

Chapter 1

Secrets to Making Money with your Camera Right Now

Secrets to Making Money Now

This chapter is really an article I wrote and published in 2011. It was so popular it got distributed to over 800 web sites worldwide. There are many fundamental principles that still apply today.

Almost every home has some kind of camera. Whether it's the popular digital cameras made by Canon, Nikon, Fugifilm or even cell phones. Anybody can learn how to make money with a camera. Now let's take a closer look at how one young man made a fortune with one photograph and a few other examples to teach you how to make money with your camera.

Upon hearing of the death of Osama Bin Laden 23 year old Maurice Haray rushed home to his apartment and put up a website selling T-shirts. He made over $120,000 in less than 2 days, by putting a photo of Osama Bin Laden on a T-shirt, and selling it on his website for $12.00 a shirt. While some in the media ran the story as if the 23 year old was lucky, I say that you create your own luck by Laboring Under Correct Knowledge. Luck is when oppurtunity mets preparation.

Secrets to Making Money Now

TAKING ACTION

Maurice got an idea and acted on it. How many of us have watched as others have prospered on ideas that we had. Belief in yourself and your ideas is a main ingredient on whether or not we decide to take action. Many successful people say that they envisioned their success long before it happened.

LABORING UNDER CORRECT KNOWLEDGE

Maurice labored under correct knowledge. This is evident in several ways. He understood marketing legend Gary Halbert's principle of hungry fish. He lived in New York and there is probably no place on earth that would be willing to purchase a Osama Bin Laden is dead t-shirt more than New York.

They were hungry for the product that he created. He also had correctly learned how to put up a website. In today's internet driven world. If you are going to maximize any chance to make money with your camera you are going to have to have some knowledge of internet marketing.

Secrets to Making Money Now

In addition his story was carried by one of the most popular entertainment shows today. So there was an element of free publicity incorporated into his marketing as well.

To get free publicity you have to create a press release and use a press release service to send the press release out to the media.

Maurice Haray got an idea, took action, and made a large sum of money in a short period of time. Sound great right! So can you. There a plenty of ways. You just have to decide and take action.

OTHER WAYS TO MAKE MONEY WITH YOUR CAMERA

You can make money with your camera by taking photos or video of special events like weddings. Banquets, graduations, and fashion shows. If you have little or no experience then you might consider working for a very low fee or for free. Just to gain experience and build up your portfolio. Contact all of your family, friend and co-workers and let them know you are willing to work for a low price or even free to gain experience. Also look in the local newspaper for knowledge of when all of the special events are taking place in your area.

Secrets to Making Money Now

MAKING NOVELTIES

Making a keychain with a photo is a fantastic novelty item you could make. There are several photos that you could make that people would love to have on their keychain. Parents always love pictures of their children. Especially when they are babies. Coffee is second only to water as the most consumed drink in the world. Photos of family on coffee mugs is another idea for making photo novelties.

IMPORTANT FAMILY EVENTS

Do you have a Navy base or port in your area? Having lived in the Norfolk Virginia area for a number of years, I can tell you the media never missed a chance to do a story on a ship either departing or coming home. There are plenty of families and couples that would love a photo of such emotional events.

Secrets to Making Money Now

BUSINESS PROFESSIONALS

There are plenty of business professionals that need to keep a current photo of themselves. Real estate agents, actors and models need to have good photos of themselves. In today's economy many are looking to cut costs, and may be more receptive to a photographer that is lower priced then their current one.

MARKETING ON A SHOESTRING BUDGET

If you are just starting out you may not have a lot of money so here are a few tips to market your new business on a shoestring budget. Make some post cards and mail them to any business that might be interested in your services. You want to mail post cards because they are less expensive and more effective than a letter. A letter might get thrown in the trash and never get read. A postcard is already open and is going to at least get glanced at before being tossed away. Then as mentioned earlier there is the internet.

I am Brian S. Mahoney and I encourage you to get a blueprint of success. Take massive action. And live your dreams.

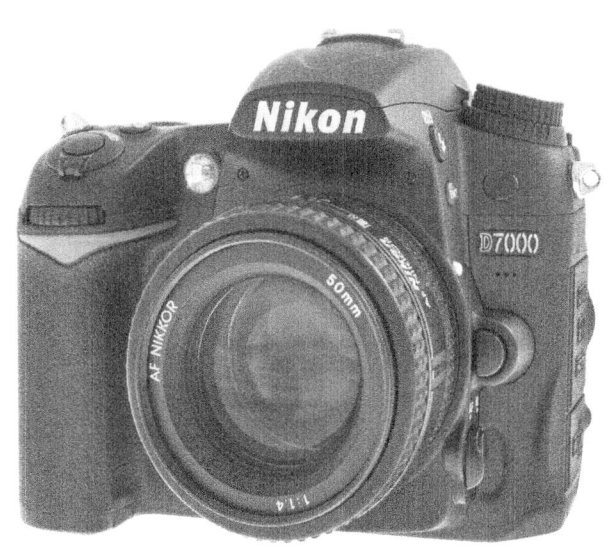

Chapter 2

Nikon D7000

Overview

NIKON D7000 OVERVIEW

Type   Digital single-lens reflex
Lens

Lens   Interchangeable, Nikon F-
mount

Sensor/Medium

Sensor   23.6 mm × 15.6 mm Nikon DX
format RGB CMOS sensor, 1.5 × FOV
crop, 4.78µm pixel size

Maximum resolution   4,928 × 3,264
(16.2 effective megapixels)

ASA/ISO range   ISO 100–6400 in 1/3
EV steps, up to 25600 with Hi (boost)
menu item

Recording medium   Secure Digital,
SDHC, SDXC compatible (Dual Slot) and
with Eye-Fi WLAN support. Supports
Ultra-High Speed (UHS-I) cards.

Focusing

Focus   Manual, Auto, Focus-lock, Electronic rangefinder,

Live preview and video modes: Subject-tracking, Face-priority, Wide-area, Normal-Area

Focus modes   Instant single-servo (AF-S); continuous-servo (AF-C); auto AF-S/AF-C selection (AF-A); Full time AF (AF-F); manual (M)

Focus areas 39-area AF system, Multi-CAM 4800DX AF Sensor Module

Area modes: 3D-tracking, Auto-area, Dynamic-area, Single-point

NIKON D7000 OVERVIEW

Exposure/Metering

Exposure modes Auto modes (auto, auto [flash off]), Advanced Scene Modes (Portrait, Landscape, Sports, Close-up, Night Portrait), programmed auto with flexible program (P), shutter-priority auto (S), aperture-priority auto (A), manual (M), quiet (Q)

Exposure metering   TTL 3D Color Matrix Metering II metering with a 2,016 pixel RGB sensor

Metering modes 3D Color Matrix Metering II, Center-weighted and Spot

NIKON D7000 OVERVIEW

Flash

Flash   Built in Pop-up, Guide number 13m at ISO 100, Standard ISO hotshoe, Compatible with the Nikon Creative Lighting System, featuring commander mode for wireless setups

Flash bracketing 2 or 3 frames in steps of 1/3, 1/2, 2/3, 1 or 2 EV

Shutter

Shutter Electronically-controlled vertical-travel focal-plane shutter

Shutter speed range   30 s to 1/8000 s in 1/2 or 1/3 stops and Bulb, 1/250 s X-sync

Continuous shooting   6 frame/s up to JPEG 100 frames or NEF 10-14 frames

NIKON D7000 OVERVIEW

Viewfinder

Optical 0.94× Pentaprism, 100% coverage

Image Processing

Custom WB Auto, Incandescent, Fluorescent, Sunlight, Flash, Cloudy, Shade, Kelvin temperature, Preset

General

Rear LCD monitor   3.0-inch 921,000 pixel (VGA x 3 colors) TFT-LCD

Battery Nikon EN-EL15 Lithium-Ion battery

Optional battery packs   Nikon MB-D11 battery grip

Weight   Approx. 690 g (1.52 lb) without battery, 780 g (1.72 lb) with battery

Made in Thailand   Sep 15, 2010

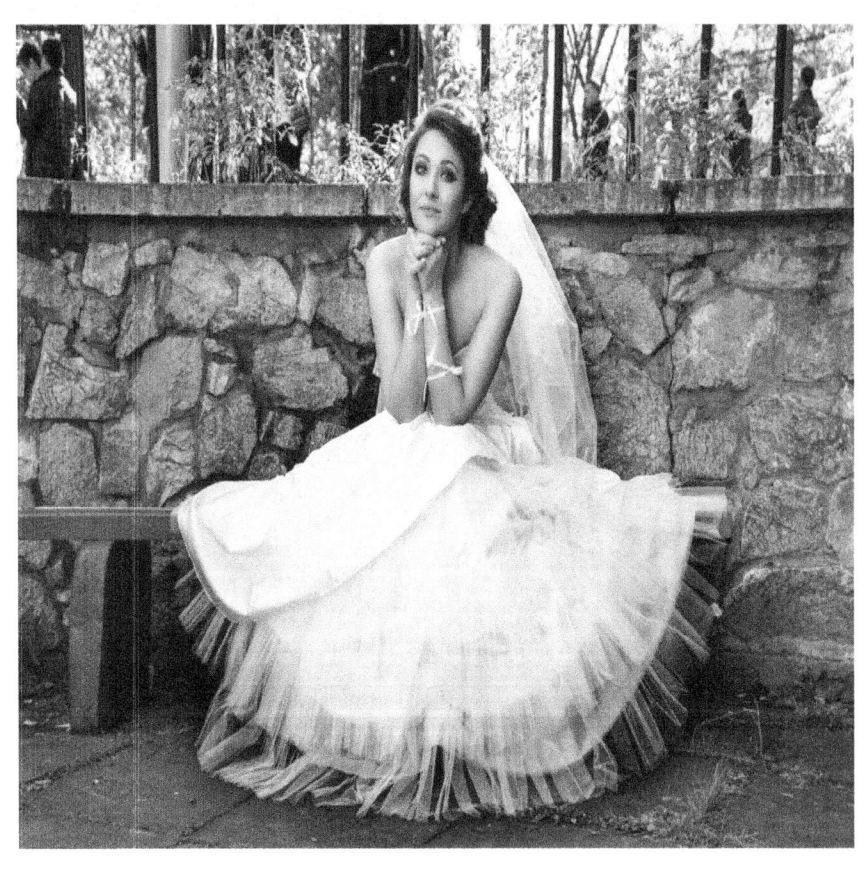

Chapter 3

Introduction to Freelancing

Introduction to Freelancing

A freelance worker is a person who seeks employment, usually on a temporary basis. Often time one short contract at a time. Sometimes a freelancer uses an agency that specializes in suppling labor for business clients or one could have their own business where work is bought to them. There are now plenty of websites that specialize in freelance work.

There are many industries that regularly use freelance workers: Computer Programmers, Writers, Web Developers, Editors, Music, Copywriters, Actors, translators, illustrators are some of the most popular fields, but the freelance industry can include many more occupations.

Introduction to Freelancing

Freelance Application

Recent statistics from a Freelance Industry so what Freelancers list as their Primary Skill:

20% Design

18% Writing

10% Editing

10% Copy writing

8% Translating

5.5% **Web Development**

4% Marketing

Over the years the freelance industry has changed. Many industries now require clients to sign contracts. A freelancer may require a deposit from a client, and may also be required to provide a documented estimate of the work, depending on the client. Some freelancers may still work for free on one project in order to get paid on another project. Each Freelance website has a different set of protocols for their freelancers and their clients.

Introduction to Freelancing

Freelance Payment

How do I get paid when I work freelance? How you get paid when you work freelance, depends on the industry that you work in. It depends on your skill level and your experience. It also depends on if you use a website to get your job or project. If you are getting your own jobs you can charge by the day, hour, rate or a per-project basis. You could also use a flat rate fee based on the market value of your work. Payment arrangements are made upfront and sometimes a percentage paid upfront is the custom, and the rest upon completion. More complex jobs may require a detailed contract with a payment schedule. One of risks of being a freelancer is that there is sometimes no guarantee of full payment.

Sometimes a writer or people in other artistic fields create work on their own and then seek a publisher for their work. They usually keep the copyright to the works and sell or license the rights to publishers in a time limited contract. Usually the work would be submitted to publishers as unsolicited query letters or manuscripts, and would get either a acceptance letter or rejection slip.

Introduction to Freelancing

When you a create intellectual property under a freelancer situation (according to the publishers' or other customers' specifications) are sometimes referred to as "independent contractors" or other similar terms.

Section 101 of the U.S. Copyright Act of 1976 (17 USC §101). Details "works made for hire", protection of intellectual property is defined.

Demographics

A new era has begun. Nine to five has defined what many people traditionally think of as a job.

Times are quickly changing. Over 53 million Americans are now earning income from jobs that are considered freelance or independent contracting. That is %33 percent of the United States workforce.

The current increase in freelance work is similar the the Industrial Revolution of times past.

The surge in freelancing is more than two decades old at this point.

Introduction to Freelancing

The freelancing increase began over twenty years ago, when with the increase in technology many more people were able to work from project to project. It was about that time that the Freelancers Union was formed by Sarah Horowitz.

About 70% of the Freelance industry is made up of women between the ages of 30 to 50. So while the regular journalism field is made up predominately of men, the freelance writing profession is mainly women.

Benefits

Freelancers have many of reasons for freelancing. The profits gained differ by gender, industry, and way of life. Recently Freelance Industry Report reported that males and females do freelance work for different reasons. Women in the survey said that they prefer the scheduling freedom and flexibility that freelancing offers, while men in the survey said they freelance to follow or pursue personal goals.

Freelancing helps people to obtain greater levels of employment in isolated communities.

Introduction to Freelancing

Workers who have been laid-off have decided to be freelancers because they can't find full-time jobs for some industries like the newspaper industry which has been declining recently. Students have become freelancers using some of their free time during the school year. Flexibility is always rated high on blogs and in interviews on websites.

Drawbacks

There are plenty of websites that specialize in Freelance work and offer plenty of advice and work for freelancers.

Freelancers usually live without job security. They also have to deal with employers who don't pay on time. Freelancers usually don't have employment benefits such as pension, sick leave, paid holidays, bonuses or health insurance.

Answers to Drawbacks

The use of freelance websites can usually eliminate the problems with payments.

Using multiple freelance websites can stockpile tons of work to add to job security.

Because you are a freelancer and your own boss, you can give yourself sick leave and paid holiday.

Introduction to Freelancing

Impact of the Internet

The power of the Internet has given the freelancer many more employment oppurtunities. There are growing markets and much more oppurtunity available for editors, writers, photographers, illustrators, graphic designers, computer program-mers, web developers and many more rising jobs.

Recent stories on CNBC and other news outlets show that online outsourcing and crowdsourcing are becoming more popular with many of the top websites like Upwork and Toptal with over a million clients. More companies are leveraging technology to fill labor shortages. Many compainies are even going outside of the United States for computer freelance work. Micro Work Sites like fiverr have become very popular.

This book will show you plenty of the top freelance websites and online marketplaces that match workers and clients using the internet. Most sites use a bidding service, fixed price or an hourly rate. Workers get paid through a merchant account supervised by the website. The website makes money by getting small percentage of each transaction.

Introduction to Freelancing

With the internet, the interview process and hiring for freelancers can be done without actually seeing the employer in person. This is amazing for being able to do long distance work all over the world. There is a drawback, because the screening process is less personal.

But the internet allows you to hire more than one person and test out their work. Fiverr is an exellent website to "test out talent" before committing to a big job. Especially for writing. With the explosion of the Amazon Kindle, many people are looking for internet writers to assist in creating content for books. With more and more blogs and webpages being put up, the demand for information technology continues to increase.

It is estimated that Amazon holds %67 of the online publishing business and %25 to Barnes and Noble. Amazon recently reported that their online electronic books have surpassed and even doubled the sales of their print books. So the need for writers has really exploided with the use of the Internet. The use of the internet and the Amazon explosion has also resulted in an increase in copy editing of book and book manuscripts and proofreading services being outsourced to freelance copy editors and proofreaders.

Introduction to Freelancing

There are many top freelancer websites. We will go into detail about the top freelancer websites in another chapter.

A few Legal aspects

For legal advice in your business consult the appropriate professional.

Some newspapers allow a writer the option of ghost signing. That is when a writer does not use their name in the byline of their article. Ghost signing allows a writer to get benefits while still being classified as a freelancer. While ghost signing is a big issue in the UK(IR35 violations) it does not matter much in the United States.

Freelancers have to handle promotion, contracts, law issues and finance and business responsibilities by themselves.

Freelancers run the risk of losing too much of their profit and have to be careful of expenses when using other professionals in their business.

The United States Federal government in 2009 began to increase their monitering of freelancers and other independent contractors.

Introduction to Freelancing

The (GAO) United States Government Accountability Office instructed the Secretary of Labor to look at freelancers or independent contractors during targeted investigations. Their targeting involves appropriate employment taxes and unemployment and workers compensation.

Chapter 4

A
Winning
Job Profile

A Winning Profile

How to create a winning profile

* Have a good headline

* Limit to one line.

* Include position title, number of years experience, specialty.

* Graphic Designer - 3 Years Experience - Photoshop

* If you are new to your profession include your top qualities.

* Use a professional looking photo.

* Blank wall with good lighting of just your head.

* Look friendly and professional.

* Make sure it is only you in the picture.

* Have a strong opening paragraph.

* Open with your qualifications.

* Tell them what makes you a good candidate.

* Look at other top profiles

- **Discuss your academic background if applicable**

A Winning Profile

* If you have a college degree or advanced degree mention that.

* Not the end of the world if you do not.

* **Use samples of your work**

* Have links to samples of your work in your portfolio.(here's were some YouTube videos can help)

* Some profiles let you attach work samples.

* Writers provide multiple articles your have written.

* Designers use links and images of designs you have done.

* If you are new this is your chance to stand out.

* **Follow rules on Freelancing sites**

* Be careful about posting your full contact details in your bids and posts.

* Some freelancing sites do not allow this.

* Use their messaging feature in that case.

* After the project is won by you, they typically give up full contact details.

* You don't want to get your profile shut down or suspended unintentionally.

A Winning Profile

Have your own website or page online about your services.

- Use "about me" to set up a free web page.

- https://about.me/

- Post your resume and links to examples of your work.

-

* Use Weebly.com for a free website.

* Use Wix.com for a free website.

Social Media Accounts

* Get active on social media.

* Facebook, Twitter, LinkedIn, GooglePlus, Pinterest

* Use a semi-professional photo on your social media profiles.

- Mention you are a freelancer on you profiles.

  -

A Winning Profile

Use Social search on Twitter

* "freelance **Your Occupation** wanted"

* "freelance **Your Occupation** needed"

* Setup Google Alerts – google.com/alerts

* So that you are the first to know about new jobs or opportunities.

* Ensures you don't miss any opportunities.

* Setup Talkwalker Alerts – talkwalker.com/alerts

*Have these sites Monitor web for keywords:

> * "freelance **Your Occupation** needed"

> * "freelance **Your Occupation** wanted"

A Winning Profile

Partner up

   * web designers and developers need content writers or copywriters in **your occupation**.

   * Marketing consultants need graphic experts.

Talk about your expertise @ clarity.fm

* Only do this if you are an expert!

* Let's you charge between $1 and $10 per minute of your time.

* This may open up additional opportunities down the line.

Bidding on Jobs Strategies

* On most freelance sites you bid on the jobs.

* Don't go for your highest rate when you start out.

* You may need to work for a discount to buildup hours worked and feedback.

* Your feedback and hours worked will make new jobs much easier.

* Work on smaller projects to build up a client base.

* Make sure you have samples of your work to present regardless of your expertise.

   • Start bidding and getting Yourself out there.

Chapter 5

The Best Job Freelancing Sites

PHOTOGRAPHY

1. Journalism.com

Open an account on the website and then use photography queries to narrow the search results.

2. freelancephotographerjobs.com

Photographer Jobs is the United States, Canada and the United Kingdom.

The Best Job Freelancing Sites

3. photography-jobs.net

Upload photos and instantly sell to millions of potential buyers.

Receive payments via Paypal, wire transfer or mailed checks.

Turn a hobby into a profitable business

4. journalismjobs.com

Just type Photographer into the search box and jobs with good descriptions come up on the landing page.

The Best Job Freelancing Sites

1. Upwork

With over 1.5 million clients and over 9 million registered users **Upwork** (formerly oDesk) likely has something for you regardless of where you are in your career. Upworkd is good for small and big projects. Upwork has hourly projects as well as per project gigs. There are entry level jobs as well as jobs for experts. This is the biggest freelancing website on the market.

Because of the massive size of this website, many of the jobs have a lot of competition which leads to low bid contests. The site also has fixed bids as well. It is a good strategy to lower your usual rate to get some jobs and build up a good reputation and rating on the site.

2. Toptal

*Unparalleled access to meaningful projects with great clients and fair compensation.

Toptal is more for freelancers with experience. Toptal has a screening process you have to pass and which leads to high level fortune 500 clients. The compensation is fair with no low bid contests. Toptal also has frequent meetups and tech events.

The Best Job Freelancing Sites

This website has been constructed for top of the line software engineers that must pass a difficult screening process. Toptal is looking for people with experience, good communication skills as well as a high level of technical know how. Toptal offers a risk free trial period. Once accepted you can set your own hourly rates.

3. Elance

As of the printing of this book (2016), the Elance website is still up, but it has merged with Upwork.

4. Freelancer

Freelancer is a big platform with lots of clients. In addition to offering millions of projects, freelancer allows you to compete with other freelancers in contests to prove your skills, showcase your abilities, and attract more clients.

If you are just starting out, because of the contests, and the large number of competitors might make this a website to try later on in your career.

The Best Job Freelancing Sites

5. Craigslist

Craigslist is more than just a website to buy & sell all types of products and people's belongings. It is a amazing source for gaining freelance employment. You can easily browse local offerings or you can search by major cities if you prefer working remotely.

While Craigslist is not a freelance only jobsite it's size makes it a great cost effective place to find freelance jobs.

6. Guru

Easily showcase your past work experience and use the daily job-matching feature to avoid missing any good opportunities.

Guru has a work room designed to let you manage all of your work, quickly and easily.

The United States was the primary target when Guru began. Now the Guru web site is worldwide and constantly expanding.

Guru primarily deals with computer programming coding but other professions are represented as well.

The Best Job Freelancing Sites

Guru has great project tracking features but also has high fees and a challenging withdrawal system, that you could incur more fees. Particularly with smaller jobs.

7. 99designs

This is a great website for freelance designers. 99designs allows you to compete in design contests and get feedback as clients choose the best ones. A great way for talented designers to prove their skills. Be careful to protect yourself from plagiarism when using this website.

8. Peopleperhour

Peopleperhour A great platform, focusing on freelancing for web projects. If you're a designer, developer, SEO specialist, etc., This site is worth checking out.

This website can have high fees and challenging customer service support.

The Best Job Freelancing Sites

9. Freelance Writing Gigs

Freelance Writing Gigs. The name almost says it all. This is a website for publishers, writers, editors, bloggers or any one who has talent with words.

10. Demand Media

Demand Media is a website for creative types to promote their talent, including writers, filmmakers, producers, **photographers**, and more.

This a a great website For Clients that need these types of creative people.

11. College Recruiter

The college student or recent graduate, often is faced with the dilemma of not having experience when searching for a job. Well, the College Recruiter website is for college students or recent graduates looking for freelance jobs of any type.

College Recruiter is a great place to get a jump on your career or earn some money doing part time work.

The Best Job Freelancing Sites

This is a website usually for smaller projects that can be done by people that do not have a lot of experience.

12. GetACoder

GetACoder is a freelancing website that focuses primarily on small projects for computer programmers, writers, web developers. This is an excellent website for freelancers that don't want to be loaded up with long term (three to six month) projects.

13. iFreelance

Unlike other sites, iFreelance is a freelancer website that allows you to keep 100% of your earnings. It accomodates writers, editors, coders, and even freelance marketers.

The Best Job Freelancing Sites

14. Project4hire

Project4hire has a ton of job categories. Easily identify jobs that suit your skillset with hundreds of project categories to choose from.

This website is primarily for computer programmers, consultants and designers. Although there are jobs for other professions.

15. SimplyHired

SimplyHired is a freelance website that is not focused on tech but has a wider range of jobs than most. This site is perfect for anyone from salespeople to construction workers.

SimplyHired has a blog with hiring tips, a company directory and location-based search. This is the perfect website for people whose skillset is not technology based.

The Best Job Freelancing Sites

16. Staff.com

Staff.com is a freelance website that is primarily for long term freelancers. Staff.com is smaller that some of the other websites in this list and gives freelancers looking for more stable work a place to go to.

17. LinkedIn

LinkedIn is a well known professional network. It features a large collectiong of resumes and professional profiles. There are many options on this website to help you increase your exposure for professional work. There are also professional courses to help you to maximize the many features on this website.

18. StackExchange

StackExchange is not a website that is dedicated to freelance workers. It does have a extremly popular Questian and Answer forum that can be used to connect with freelance or independent contractors and employers. It could take more work than other websites, but is still a place were a freelancer can network to get a job.

The Best Job Freelancing Sites

19. Jobs.smashingmagazine.com

An excellent portal for developers and designers to find freelance jobs.

20. FLEXJOBS.COM

This freelance website stands out by vetting jobs, not freelancers. In return, flexjobs provides a job list of just under 30,000 projects with contact information.

Whether you are a computer programmer, web designer, experienced, or just out of college or something in between, there is a freelance platform out there for you.

This website also has skill testing and job search tips.

21. virtualvocations.com/jobs

Virtual Vocations is a job service that provides job-seekers with hand-screened telecommuting jobs leads that offer real pay for real work. From account management to writing, all of the job openings we bring you offer some form of telecommuting or virtual work.

Chapter 6

Basic

Photography

Equipment

Needed

Basic Photography Equipment Needed

The basic photography equipment needed chapter shows you the basic equipment that is needed to start your photography business, and where to find it.

Web Pages and product offers expire, so most of the info for equipment needed has multiple links to find it. I also did price comparisons to get the lowest price possible in most cases. That is why a few of the prices are listed as sale price. Products are:

1. Backdrop stands

2. Card Readers

3. Clamps

4. Lenses

5. Lights

6. Memory cards

7. Multi Disk Reflector

8. Octoadom photo flex

9. Photography Umbrella

10. Strobe Lights

11. Tripods

12. Universal speed ring

Basic Photography Equipment Needed

1. Backdrop stands

ebay.com

Abs Photo's Video Backdrop Stand Kit 10 Tall x 12.3 Wide With Dual Air Cushion

$83.31

https://goo.gl/nE8Vbc

efavormart.com

10ft x 10ft Adjustable Heavy Duty Pipe and Drape Kit Backdrop Support with Weighted Steel Base   Item Number: BKDP_STND07

$139.99   Sale Price $202.99   Retail Price

https://goo.gl/Jh2yyA

Aceexhibits

FlexDrop Adjustable Backdrop Stand $440.00

https://goo.gl/XbdtWS

Basic Photography Equipment Needed

2. Card Readers

Transcend USB 3.0 Multi Card Reader - White #TS-RDF8W

$12.00

https://goo.gl/X1SMA6

Lexar Professional LRW400 Dual Slot SD & CF Reader

$34.95

https://goo.gl/M6QfHL

Kingston Technology USB 3.0 Hi-Speed Memory Card Media Reader Writer #FCR-HS4

$17.99

https://goo.gl/vRkuEg

Basic Photography Equipment Needed

3. Clamps

Clamps are needed in photography for tightening up clothes, hanging backdrop to holding heavy equipment. Here are the types of clamps most used in photography.

"A" Clamps

PJ Tool

https://goo.gl/NpJLdU

Home Depot

https://goo.gl/hrijxK

Super Clamp

BHPhotoVideo

https://goo.gl/wnfAmC

Adorama

https://www.adorama.com/fpxcp06k4.html

Basic Photography Equipment Needed

Cardellini Clamp

Cardelliniclamp

http://www.cardelliniclamp.com/

Platypus Clamp

Home Depot

https://goo.gl/VS9d5Q

Hardwarefy

http://www.hardwarefy.com/truper-sheet-metal-welding-locking-pliers-8-17425/

"C" Clamp

Stagelightingstore

https://goo.gl/5K7QxW

Grainger

https://goo.gl/hrvbx3

Basic Photography Equipment Needed

Chain Vice Grip

Home Depot

https://goo.gl/dkDYnJ

Zoro

https://goo.gl/D8jhtN

Basic Photography Equipment Needed

4. Lenses

Sigma 17-50mm f/2.8 EX DC OS HSM Auto Focus Wide Angle Zoom Lens for Nikon Digital SLR Cameras $279.00

The Sigma 17-50mm is commonly used for Landscape/scenery, Low light, Night photography, Sports/action, Video, Weddings and more.The Sigma 17-50mm is most used by customers who consider themselves to be a Casual photographer, Photo enthusiast, Semi-pro photographer among others.

The Sigma 17-50mm is popular because customers like the following qualities of the Sigma 17-50mm: Consistent output, Durable, Easily interchangeable, Fast / accurate auto-focus, Lightweight, Nice bokeh, Rugged and Strong construction.

Basic Photography Equipment Needed

Sigma 17-50mm (cont)

For use with smaller chip APS-c or 4/3 digital cameras only.

Offers Sigma's OS System (Optical Stabilization) allowing handheld photography even in low-light situation.

HSM (Hyper-Sonic Motor) ensures a quiet & high-speed auto focus.

FLD glass elements with performance equal to fluorite glass for compensate for color aberration

Ultra compact with overall length of just 3.6"

https://goo.gl/HNHJTH

Basic Photography Equipment Needed

Sigma 50mm f/1.4 DG HSM ART Lens for Sony Alpha & Maxxum DSLR Cameras Features $599.00

The Sigma 50mm F1.4 DG HSM Art is a pro-level performer for full-frame DSLRs and is ideal for many types of videography and photography, including portraits, landscapes, studio work and still-life. It has been redesigned and re-engineered with SLD glass and has been optimized for rich peripheral brightness, with improved large aperture performance by positioning wide elements into the front groups.

Completely redesigned and reengineered

Exceptional Image Quality

Incredible focal point sharpness when wide open

Pairs well with Pro-Level DSLR's

MTF A1-tested

https://goo.gl/CCcJnY

Basic Photography Equipment Needed

5. Lights

Docooler Portable Video Studio Photography Light Lamp Panel 176 LEDs 5600K for DSLR Camera ($24.99)

Designed with 176pcs LEDs, high brightness. Small size and light weight, very convenient for indoor and outdoor photography. It is an ideal companion for professional photographer and enthusiast.

With 176pcs high-quality LED beads, output high brightness, 5600K color temperature.

Comes with 2 color temperature plates (white and orange), for replacement to soften the light.

LED display design, make it easier for you to get accurate brightness value (from 10 to 99).

Supports external direct-current power input and battery power supply. (Not included)

With 1/4" screw hole in the bottom and comes with an 1/4" adapter, very easy to install on the tripod, DV and camera.

Small size and light-weight, very convenient for carrying.

https://goo.gl/s2MXbY

Basic Photography Equipment Needed

Viltrox VL-162T Professional Bi-Color Dimmable LED Video Light $31.98

With Digital LCD Panel / 3300K-5600K 12W CRI 95+ / for Canon Nikon Sony DSLR Camera Camcorder

Brand: VILTROX

Model: VL-162T

Color Temperature: 3300K~5600K (can be adjusted)

Brightness Range: 20%~100% (can be adjusted)

Max. Brightness/ Illumination: 1070LM / 1250Lux (1m)

Power: 12W

Continued Light Time: Approx. 3 hours (100% full, Li-battery NP-F550/F960 series)

Color Rendering Index: ≥95 (RA)

Basic Photography Equipment Needed

Viltrox VL-162T Professional Bi-Color Dimmable LED Video Light

Input Power: DC 9V~12V/1.5A, DC005 general interface

Item Size: 16.8 * 9.8 * 3.2cm / 6.6 * 3.9 * 1.3in

Item Weight: 226g / 8oz

Package Size: 25.3 * 13.9 * 5.7cm / 10 * 5.5 * 2.2in

Package Weight: 420g / 14.8oz

Package List:

1 * LED video light

1 * White Filter Panel

1 * Hot shoe adapter

1 * User manual (English & Chinese)

https://goo.gl/pL2wrE

Basic Photography Equipment Needed

Aputure AL-M9 Amaran Pocket-Sized Daylight-Balanced LED Light $45.00

The Amaran AL-M9 is a LED fill light so small it fits in your pocket. It's compact and incedibly lightweight with 9 SMD bulbs that are powerful in the palm of your hand. It provides a max of 900lux that is able to do close-up fill light. You can use this light for a wide variety of applications to quick moving video to macro product photography, promising unlimited potential for how you can use this light.

- High Efficiency Bulbs, TLCI 95+

- 9 SMD light beads, Creating High illuminance

- Built-in Lithium Battery, Charged via USE3

- Ultra Thin with Only 140g Weight

- Adjustable Brightness in 9 steps

https://goo.gl/wmifvU

Basic Photography Equipment Needed

6. 64GB Memory Cards

Transcend 64GB SDXC Ultimate Class 10 UHS-1 Memory Card, 90MB/s Max Transfer Rate $40.99

https://www.adorama.com/tssdxc10u164.html

Lexar 64GB Professional Class 10 UHS-I U1 633x SDXC Memory Card, Up to 95MB/s Read, Up to 20MB/s Write

$28.00

https://goo.gl/EnkxeP

SanDisk Extreme PRO 64GB UHS-I Class 10 U3 V30 SDXC Memory Card

$36.00

https://goo.gl/44oi8J

Basic Photography Equipment Needed

7. Multi Disk Reflector

ebay.com

110CM 43" 5-in-1 Photography Studio Multi Photo Disc Collapsible Light Reflector

$20.88   Free Shipping

https://goo.gl/GVz4BG

bhphotovideo.com

Photoflex MultiDisc 5-in-1 Reflector (22") B&H # PHMD22 MFR # 870220

https://goo.gl/PZUW9V

Google Express

International Square Perfect Collapsible 43-Inch 5-in-1 Light Photo Disc Reflector (Set of 5) (2811 SP-43 5in1 Disc), Yellow Sunshine

https://goo.gl/7QKVUT

Basic Photography Equipment Needed

8. Octoadom photo flex

bhphotovideo

Photoflex Inner Diffusion Baffle for Medium OctoDome Softbox $17.95

https://goo.gl/ZJnto4

9. Photography Umbrella

Cameta Camera

Photoflex 45" Convertible White Satin Umbrella with Removable Black Cover

Our Price: $39.95

https://goo.gl/pgU75r

Best Buy

Insignia™ - 33" Dual-Layer Umbrella - White/Silver/Black $14.99

https://goo.gl/hD5k2Z

Basic Photography Equipment Needed

Efavormart

10Ft Background Support System, 600W 6500K White Umbrella Lighting Photo Video Studio Kit With Chromakey Background Muslins (Green Black White) - Free Carry Case

Item Number: PHOTO_LGT_006

$121.78Sale Price   **$176.58   Retail Price**

https://goo.gl/6nh4ip

Basic Photography Equipment Needed

10. Strobe Lights

Westcott Strobelite, 150 Watt Second Monolight with 100 Watt Modeling Light $149.90

The Wescott Strobelight features 150 watt/second capability and a recycle time of 2 seconds at full power. Lightweight, durable and inexpensive, the Wescott Strobelight is an effective solution for studio shooting.

Product Highlights

150Ws

120 VAC

2.5 Second Recycling @ Full Power

Reflector, Mini to PC Sync Cord

https://goo.gl/Wqz6Z1

Basic Photography Equipment Needed

Dynalite Baja B4 Battery-Powered Monolight $599.00

Product Highlights

2.4 GHz Power Control Wireless Receiver

400Ws, 6-Stop Power Range

1/10 Stop Power Increments

Rechargeable Li-Ion Battery Power

Up to 550 Full-Power Flashes

Flash Duration: 1/12800 - 1/500 Sec

LED Modeling Light

Built-In Optical Slave

C-Mode for up to 15 Flashes per Second

Bowens Accessory Mount

https://goo.gl/8jiocK

Basic Photography Equipment Needed

Dynalite Wireless Transmitter for Baja B4 Monolight $63.00

The Wireless Transmitter for Baja B4 Monolight from Dynalite allows wireless triggering of the Baja, as well as power level control at distances up to 590'. Operating on the 2.4 GHz frequency, the hot shoe style transmitter offers 6 separate groups with 16 channels and flash syncs as short as 1/250 sec. This transmitter will not give you High Speed Sync. To take advantage of HSS Canon users need to purchase a dedicated DYBRT616C Transmitter. Nikon users need to purchase a dedicated BYBRT616N Transmitter and also a DYBRR616N dedicated receiver to replace the one that comes with the Baja.

Frequency 2.4 GHz

Range   590' (180 m)

Channels and Groups   16 Channels, 6 groups

Flash Sync 1/250 Sec.

Power   1x AA battery (included)

Packaging Info   Package Weight   0.35

Box Dimensions (HxWxD)   2.5 x 4.0 x 6.0

https://goo.gl/Pp1KHq

Basic Photography Equipment Needed

11. Tripod

Crutchfield.com

Nikon Prostaff Full Size Tripod Item # 054847 | MFR # 847 $52.95

https://goo.gl/UnA7GJ

Walmart online

72" Pro Portable DV Video Camera Tripod Steady Stand Fluid Damping Head Kit w/ Bag 33lbs Capacity $104.95   List $214.90   Save $109.95

https://goo.gl/4MivnT

Jet.com

72 In. Pro Portable Aluminum DV Video Camera Tripod Stand Fluid Pan Head Kit w/ Carring Bag

https://goo.gl/bmED9M

Basic Photography Equipment Needed

12. Universal speed ring

Newegg.com

Loadstone Studio Photography Softbox Universal Speed Ring For Photo Studio Lighting, NE_LI1067 $16.20

https://goo.gl/XPkdAw

Walmart

Fotodiox Softbox Universal Speedring Speed Ring and Plate for Strobe Lights - Fits 3-6in Diameter Strobe Heads $19.95

https://goo.gl/z73YTY

Chapter 7

Get Long Term Business Success with Email Marketing

Email Marketing

Email Marketing overview

Email marketing is now the key to long term success to just about any business. More and more major corporations are doing what ever it takes to get you to give them your email address. Why? Because email marketing is often times close to free and can be extremely effective if done correctly.

There are several components to email marketing:

* Select a profitable Niche to Market to.

* Create a compelling Free Offer

* Create a product to give for free

* Create a Squeeze or Landing Page to store the Email Addresses

* Get a Autoresponder to send out the responses

* Generate massive traffic to your Squeeze page

* Don't stop until you build a large mailing list

In this chapter we are going to cover all of the components of building a customer list at zero cost to you.

Email Marketing

Select a profitable niche market

The first thing you have to do is choose a niche market to target. A niche market is a group of people with a common interest or problem. The more specific the niche the higher response rate you will have to your offers. Don't spend a long time doing niche research.

You don't have to be an expert in the niche you choose. You do need to know where to find the experts to create a compelling offer.

There are plenty of places you can go to help you decide what niche you want to target. One place is www.magazines.com if there is a magazine for it, there is a group of people that enjoy that topic.

Email Marketing

Here are some popular niches in the photography business:

architectural

cinematography

collections catalogues & exhibitions

color

criticism & essays

darkroom & processing

digital photography

equipment

Erotica

Fashion

History

Lighting

Nature & Wildlife

Photojournalism

Portraits & Selfies

Travel

Email Marketing

Creating Your Free Offer

To get people to optin to your mailing list, you have to create a free offer. Some refer to this as an ethical bribe. Even though your offer is free, it still has to be a compelling offer. Jeff Walker the creator of Product Lauch Formula is considered by many to be the "Grand Poobah" of email marketing. He once said "the 2nd best product launch program on the market is the one I give away for free. The best one on the market is the one people purchase from me."

So when you are creating a free product give away, make sure that it is a quality product, the people will be compelled to give you their email address to obtain it.

Here are some ideas for product creation:

A free report on your niche. (about 7 -15 pages) Could be a link to your blog or web page.

A link to a set of quality YouTube videos about your niche.

A link to a set of YouTube video you create about your niche.

A series of articles about your niche.

A PDF book about your niche.

Email Marketing

You would use your autoresponder to send these links to your subscribers.

If you create a PDF you can have these web sites host the PDF for download.

www.slideshare.net   www.edocr.com

The web sites listed above are currently free document sharing web sites.

There are plenty of places you can use to do research for the content in your product. Some of my favorites are Wikipedia, YouTube and Ezinearticles.

If you don't want to create a product yourself, you can go to www.fiverr.com and contract the work out for as little as $5.

Email Marketing

Autoresponder Service

A autoresponder is a program that automatically generates a set response to all messages sent to a particular email address. To collect your leads and respond to them, you need a autoresponder service. Two free autoresponder services are sendfree.com and listwire.com. Listwire is the more popular of the two but if you decide to use a free service you can test them both out.

Once you select your autoresponder service you have to setup your follow up message to go to your subscribers. Your first message should link to the optin report or gift you promised. Your second message should presell the product or offer you are promoting.

Space your messages a day or two apart. Build a relationship:

* Let your subscribers know who you are.

* Let them know you understand what they are going through.

* Let them know how you can resolve any challenges they have.

* Create a really good free offer to help establish trust.

Email Marketing

By capturing your buyer's email address is just the beginning to creating a more sustainable business. You have to cultivate the relationship by giving quality service and products to your subscribers.

Set up your landing page

Landing Page - the section of a website accessed by clicking a hyperlink on another web page, typically the website's home page. A squeeze page is a landing page designed to capture opt-in email addresses from potential subscribers. The goal of a squeeze page is to convince, cajole, or otherwise "squeeze" a visitor into providing one of their most sought-after and coveted pieces of personal data: the email address.

You need a web host for your landing page. The top free web hosting sites are

https://www.weebly.com/ and https://www.wix.com/ . Here is an example of a squeeze page using wix.

https://mahoneyproducts.wixsite.com/win1

Email Marketing

Your free landing page should describe your free offer accurately encourage them to optin to receive your free offer. Start with a good attention getting headline.

Here is a better example of a squeeze page that uses bullet points to describe the value they will get from your offer and the benefit to them.

http://www.plrcounts.com/

Keep the page as short as possible once you generate some money scale up and use paid web hosting web sites like...

godaddy.com

hostgator.com

bluehost.com

You can also scale up your autoresponder service with:

aweber.com

getresponse.com

Setting up a good landing page takes time, but once it's done, it can give your business a long term data base of customers for the life time of your business.

Email Marketing

Getting Traffic to your landing page

Traffic is the currency of online business. Here are some ways that you can send massive traffic to any and all of your offers.

YouTube

YouTube has a billion users. The potential to capture the imagination of your niche market is wonderful with YouTube. In an interview with Charlie Rose, the founder of Wikipedia made it clear that you can use the content from Wikipedia for free, without fear of copywrite violations. You now have a complete library of information to create YouTube videos.

Complete YouTube Training Course:

 https://goo.gl/TdBdP2

Email Marketing

Video Marketing

Create and submit videos to video sharing sites like dailymotion.com or youtube.com. Make sure to include a hyperlink to your website, product or service in the description of your videos.

Create an account with YouTube.com. Research keywords for your video tags. You can research keywords at https://www.seocentro.com/ . The tags represent the words users will type to find your video. The key is to outrank your competition that is using the same keywords.

One way to outrank your competiton is to create other social media accounts and link your videos to those accounts.

After you upload your video, watch it on the YouTube channel (not the editing portion) and there is a "share" button. Press the button and link to your other social media accounts. Below is a list of accounts that the "share" button accesses.

Email Marketing

Facebook

https://www.facebook.com/

Pinterest

https://www.pinterest.com/

Digg

http://digg.com/

Tumblr

https://www.tumblr.com/

Linkedin

https://www.linkedin.com/

Twitter

https://twitter.com/

Google Plus

https://plus.google.com/

Email Marketing

Writing and submitting a Press Release

Write and submit a press release. A press release has a basic format that should be followed if you want any one in the media to accept and publish it.

The top of the press release should have your contact information and For Immediate Release or a date for release.

A press release should be written like a news worthy story, not a ad for your business, product or service.

https://www.yahoo.com/news/former-addict-opens-gym-help-205337003.html

Above is a perfect example of a person promoting their gym and gofundme page, by creating a "news worthy" story. Most of the media outlets that ran the story allowed hyperlinks to promote the gym and funding. She literally got millions of dollars of free publicity. If a drug addict can do it. You can do it.

Your press release should have an attention getting title. Most media people are busy and have hundreds, if not thousands of press releases to sort through. You must get their attendtion with a compelling headline.

Email Marketing

The first paragraph should be one or two sentences and summarize the topic.

Example: The Revolutionary War

Summary: The Colonies fought the British, they lost.

The second paragraph credentializes you and goes into detail about your topic.

The third paragraph is your summary and call to action. "For more information visit www.yourwebsite.com

Every press release should end with a ### symbol at the bottom of the page.

When you select a website to submit your press release to, view press releases that have already been published to get an idea of how to write and format them.

Free Press Release Sites

https://www.free-press-release-center.info/

http://www.free-press-release.com/

If you don't want to write a press release you can contract out the work for as little as $5.00 at www.fiverr.com.

Email Marketing

Article Marketing

Write and submit articles to article marketing web sites like ezinearticles.com.

When writing your article you write between 700 and 800 words. This is the size the lot's of blogs and other websites prefer.

Most article marketing web hosts allow 1 or 2 hyperlinks to be placed in the article.

Top Article Submission Websites

http://ezinearticles.com/

https://www.articlesbase.com/

http://www.articles.org/

Email Marketing

Amazon.com

Amazon has a book category call short reads. Here is a link to their 15 minute 1-11 page book, short read category of best sellers. Use the list of best sellers to get an idea of what to create. Keep in mind there are several short read categories to choose from.

https://goo.gl/Zg2JYp

https://www.amazon.com/Best-Sellers-Kindle-Store-15-Minute-Arts-Photography-Short-Reads/zgbs/digital-text/8624102011/ref=zg_bs_nav_kstore_3_8584458 011

Join Amazon's Kindle book publishing program.

https://kdp.amazon.com/

Create a short read book and upload it to Amazon.com. Amazon allows you to place your book for free for 5 days, every 90 day period.

Email Marketing

Place a link to your product, service or offer in your short read book. Place the book on Amazon for free. Hire a kindle book promoter from fiverr.com. Always set the dates for free downloads, 1 week from promotion, to give a promoter time set everything up.

Just go to fiverr.com and type book promotion. I have used a promoter by the name of "bknights". However at the time of this writing he has 203 jobs in his que. There are plenty of inexpensive book promoters on this site to choose from.

You must be consistant with your traffic promotion. One video, one press release, one article is not going to make you rich. You have to do several of each to establish a good flow of traffic. Whatever form of promotion you choose, look at your competition and get ideas from those that are doing the very best.

Chapter 8

Getting Started in Business

Step by Step

Getting Started in Business

There are over thirty million home-based businesses in the United States alone.

Many people dream of the independence and financial reward of having a home business. Unfortunately they let analysis paralysis stop them from taking action. This chapter is designed to give you a road map to get started. The most difficult step in any journey is the first step.

Anthony Robbins created a program called Personal Power. I studied the program a long time ago, and today I would summarize it, by saying you must figure out a way to motivate yourself to take massive action without fear of failure. Usually that way is giving yourself powerful whys.

2 Timothy 1:7 King James Version

"For God hath not given us the spirit of fear; but of power, and of love, and of a sound mind."

Getting Started in Business

STEP #1 MAKE AN OFFICE IN YOUR HOUSE

If you are serious about making money, then redo the man cave or the woman's cave and make a place for you to do business, uninterupted.

STEP #2 BUDGET OUT TIME FOR YOU BUSINESS

If you already have a job, or if you have children, then they can take up a great deal of your time. Not to mention well meaning friends who use the phone to become time theives. Budget time for your business and stick to it.

STEP #3 DECIDE ON THE TYPE OF BUSINESS

You don't have to be rigid, but begin with the end in mine. You can become more flexible as you gain experience.

STEP #4 LEGAL FORM FOR YOUR BUSINESS

The three basic legal forms are sole proprietorship, partnership, and corporation. Each one has it's advantages.

Go to

https://www.sba.gov/business-guide/launch-your-business/choose-business-structure

https://goo.gl/LJMWNK

and learn about each and make a decision.

STEP #5 PICK A BUSINESS NAME AND REGISTER IT

One of the safest ways to pick a business name is to use your own name. Your own name is not copywrited.

However, always check with an Attorney or the proper legal authority when dealing with legal matters.

STEP #6 WRITE A BUSINESS PLAN

This would seem like a no brainer. No matter what you are trying to accomplish you should have a blueprint. You should have a business plan. In the NFL about seven headcoaches get fired every season. So in a very competetive business, a man with no head coaching experience got hired by the NFL's Philadelphia Eagles. His name was Andy Reid. Andy Reid would later become one of the most successful coaches in the team's history. One of the reasons the owner Jeffrey Lurie hired him, was because he had a business plan the size of a telephone book. Your business plan does not need to be nearly that big, but if you plan for as many things as possible, you are less likely to get rattled when things don't go as planned.

STEP #7 PROPER LICENSES & PERMITS

Go to city hall and find out what you need to do, to start a home business.

STEP #8 SELECT BUSINESS CARDS, STATIONERY, BROCHURES

This is one of the least expensive ways to not only start your business but to promote and network your business.

STEP #9 OPEN A BUSINESS CHECKING ACCOUNT

Having a separate business account makes it much easier to keep track of profit and expenses. This will come in very handy, whether you decide to do your own taxes or hire out an professional.

STEP #10 TAKE SOME SORT OF ACTION TODAY!

This is not meant to be a comprehensive plan to start a business. It is meant to point you in the right direction to get started. You can go to the Small Business Administration for many free resources for starting your business. They even have a program(SCORE) that will give you access to many retired professionals who will advise you for free!
www.score.org

Chapter 9

Small Business Grants

How to write a Winning Grant Proposal

Small Business Grants

Government grants. Many people either don't believe government grants exist or they don't think they would ever be able to get government grant money.

First lets make one thing clear. Government grant money is **YOUR MONEY**. Government money comes from taxes paid by residents of this country. Depending on what state you live in, you are paying taxes on almost everything....Property tax for your house. Property tax on your car. Taxes on the things you purchase in the mall, or at the gas station. Taxes on your gasoline, taxes the food you buy etc.

So get yourself in the frame of mind that you are not a charity case or too proud to ask for help, because billionaire companies like GM, Big Banks and most of Corporate America is not hesitating to get their share of **YOUR MONEY**!

There are over two thousand three hundred (2,300) Federal Government Assistance Programs. Some are loans but many are formula grants and project grants. To see all of the programs available go to:

http://www.CFDA.gov

Small Business Grants

https://www.sbir.gov/

SBIR

The Small Business Innovation Research (SBIR) program is a program that has a lot of competition.

It encourages small businesses that exist inside the United States, to participate in Federal Research/Research and Development (R/R&D) that has the potential for financial gain.

Through a competitive awards-based program, Small Business Innovation Research program gives small businesses the opportunity to search for and reach their technological potential and provides the incentive to profit from its application to business.

By including qualified small businesses in the nation"s R&D arena, we encourage interest in high-tech innovation and the country gains the entrepreneurial spirit as it meets its specific research and development needs.

Small Business Grants

WRITING A GRANT PROPOSAL

The Basic Components of a Proposal

There are eight basic components to creating a solid proposal package:

1. The proposal summary;

2. Introduction of organization;

3. The problem statement   (or needs assessment);

4. Project objectives;

5. Project methods or design;

6. Project evaluation;

7. Future funding; and

8. The project budget.

Small Business Grants

The Proposal Summary

The Proposal Summary is an outline of the project goals and objectives. Keep the Proposal Summary short and to the point. No more than 2 or 3 paragraphs. Put it at the beginning the proposal.

Introduction

The Introduction portion of your grant proposal presents you and your business as a credible applicant and organization.

Highlight the accomplishments of your organization from all sources: newspaper or online articles etc. Include a biography of key members and leaders. State the goals and philosophy of the company.

The Problem Statement

The problem statement makes clear the problem you are going to solve(maybe reduce homelessness). Make sure to use facts. State who and how those affected will benefits from solving the problem. State the exact manner in how you will solve the problem.

Small Business Grants

Project Objectives

The Project Objectives section of your grant proposal focuses on the Goals and Desired outcome.

Make sure to indentify all objectives and how you are going to reach these objectives. The more statistics you can find to support your objectives the better. Make sure to put in realistic objectives. You may be judged on how well you accomplish what you said you intended to do.

Program Methods and Design

The program methods and design section of your grant proposal is a detailed plan of action.

What resources are going to be used.

What staff is going to be needed.

System development

Create a Flow Chart of project features.

Explain what will be achieved.

Try to produce evidence of what will be achieved.

Make a diagram of program design.

Small Business Grants

Evaluation

There is product evaluation and process evaluation. The product evaluation deals with the result that relate to the project and how well the project has met it's objectives.

The process evaluation deals with how the project was conducted, how did it line up the original stated plan and the overall effectiveness of the different aspects of the plan.

Evaluations can start at anytime during the project or at the project's conclusion. It is advised to submit a evaluation design at the start of a project.

 It looks better if you have collected convincing data before and during the program.

If evaluation design is not presented at the beginning that might encourage a critical review of the program design.

Future Funding

The Future Funding part of the grant proposal should have long term project planning past the grant period.

Small Business Grants

Budget

Utilities, rental equipment, staffing, salary, food, transportation, phone bills and insurance are just some of the things to include in the budget.

A well constructed budget accounts for every penny.

A complete guide for government grants is available at the website link below.

https://www.cfda.gov/downloads/CFDA.GOV_Public_User_Guide_v2.0.pdf

The guide can also be accessed at the very bottom of every page of the https://www.cfda.gov/ website.

Small Business Grants

Other sources of Government Funding

Get $500 to 5.5 Million to fund your business!

There are loans guaranteed by the Small Business Administration that range from $500 to $5,000,000 and can be used for almost any business purpose. Long-term fixed assets and operating capital. Some loan programs do have restrictions on how you can use the funds, so see a SBA-approved lender when you are requesting a loan. The lender can match you with the correct loan for your business needs.

To get General Small Business loans from the government. Go to the Small Business Administration for more information.

https://www.sba.gov/funding-programs/loans

SBA Microloan Program

The Microloan program provides loans of up to $50,000 with the average loan being $13,000.

https://www.sba.gov/

Chapter 10

Zero Cost
Business Launch
Formula

ZERO COST LAUCH FORMULA

The Million Dollar Rolodex has plenty of web sites for you to find products at huge dicounts. Below are a few steps to marketing your business, products or service using ZERO COST INTERNET MARKETING stratigies.

While there are many ways to market we are only going focus on ZERO COST MARKETING. You are starting up. You can always go for the more expensive ways of marketing after your business is producing income.

FREE WEB HOSTING

Get a free web site. You can get a free web site at weebly.com or wix.com. Or just type "free web hosting" in a google, bing or yahoo search engine.

Free web hosting is something you can use for a varitey or reasons. However many free web hosting sites add an extention to the name of you web address that lets everyone know you are using their services. For this reason you eventually want to scale up once you start making income.

ZERO COST LAUCH FORMULA

LOW COST PAID WEB HOSTING

Free is nice, but you when you need to expand your business it is best to go with a paid web hosting service. There are several that give you good value for under $10.00 a month.

1. Yahoo small business

2. Intuit.com

3. ipage.com

4. Hostgator.com

5. Godaddy.com

Yahoo small business allows for unlimited web pages and is probably the best overall value, but they require a years payment up front. Intuit allows for monthly payments.

ZERO COST LAUCH FORMULA

Getting Paid

Lot's of web hosting platforms have a monthly service charge for you to accept payment from your customers.

For free ecommerce on your web site, open up a free Paypal account and get the HTML code for payment buttons for free. Then put those buttons on your web site.

Creating a Paypal payment button.

Log into your Paypal account. At the top of the page select the "Tools" pull down menu. Select "All Tools".

Go to PayPal buttons and click **Open**. Select the "Buy Now" payment button. Fill in the product information and press "Create Button".

ZERO COST LAUCH FORMULA

Step 1 Register Your Web Site.

Now that your web site is up and running you should register it with at least the top 3 search engines. Being indexed in search engines is not always automatic. If you are not indexed you can't be found in search results.

Google

Add your URL to Google by using the link below.

https://goo.gl/F6oi7N

Bing

Add your URL to Bing by using the link below.

https://www.bing.com/toolbox/submit-site-url

Yahoo

Add your URL to Yahoo by using the link below.

https://search.yahoo.com/info/submit.html

ZERO COST LAUCH FORMULA

Step 2 Writing and submitting a Press Release

Write and submit a **press release**. A press release has to a basic format that should be followed if you want any one in the media to accept and publish it.

The top of the press release should have your contact information and For Immediate Release or a date for release.

A press release should be written like a news worthy story, not a ad for your business, product or service.

Your press release should have an attention getting title. Most media people are busy and have hundreds, if not thousands of press releases to sort through. You must get their attendtion with a compelling headline.

The first paragraph should be one or two sentences and summarize the topic.

Example: The Revolutionary War

Summary: The Colonies fought the British, they lost.

The second paragraph credentializes you and goes into detail about your topic.

ZERO COST LAUCH FORMULA

Writing and submitting a Press Release

The third paragraph is your summary and call to action. "For more information visit www.yourwebsite.com

Every press release should end with a ### symbol at the bottom of the page.

When you select a website to submit your press release to, view press releases that have already been published to get an idea of how to write and format them.

Free Press Release Sites

https://www.free-press-release-center.info/

http://www.free-press-release.com/

If you don't want to write a press release you can contract out the work for as little as $5.00 at www.fiverr.com.

ZERO COST LAUCH FORMULA

Step 3 Article Marketing

Write and submit articles to article marketing web sites like **ezinearticles.com.**

When you use a article marketing website, you are submitting an article that can be picked up for free to provide content to websites all over the world! In exchange you get exposure. Usually in the form of a hyperlink that leads back to your website, video or sales page.

I can tell you from experience as many as half of the content borrowers out there will eliminate your hyperlink & name and claim the article for themselves. It is part of doing business with free services.

Writing a article is similar to writing a press release in the sense that you are not writing an ad for your business, product or service. Instead you are giving valuable information about your business, product or service.

When writing your article you write between 700 and 800 words. This is the size the lot's of blogs and other websites prefer.

ZERO COST LAUCH FORMULA

Top Article Submission Websites

http://ezinearticles.com/

https://www.articlesbase.com/

http://www.articles.org/

http://www.articlesfactory.com/

http://www.sooperarticles.com/

https://www.articlecube.com/

http://articles.pubarticles.com/

ZERO COST LAUCH FORMULA

Step 4 Video Marketing

Create and submit videos to video sharing sites like dailymotion.com or **youtube.com.** Make sure to include a hyperlink to your website in the description of your videos.

YouTube recently changed their monetization rules. In the past you could create an account, post videos and get paid for allowing ads to play before your videos. Now you must have at least 1,000 subscribers and 4,000 hours viewed in the past 12 months in order to get paid from the Google adsense program for your videos. However you can still make money from YouTube by placing a hyperlink in the description portion of your video and send traffic to your website, sales page or product or service offer.

Create an account with YouTube.com. Research keywords for your video tags. The tags represent the words users will type to find your video. The key is to outrank your competition that is using the same keywords.

One way to outrank your competiton is to create other social media accounts and link your videos to those accounts.

ZERO COST LAUCH FORMULA

After you upload your video, watch it on the YouTube channel (not the editing portion) and there is a "share" button. Press the button and link to your other social media accounts. Below is a list of accounts that the "share" button accesses.

Facebook

https://www.facebook.com/

Pinterest

https://www.pinterest.com/

Digg

http://digg.com/

Tumblr

https://www.tumblr.com/

Linkedin

https://www.linkedin.com/

Twitter

https://twitter.com/

Google Plus

https://plus.google.com/

ZERO COST LAUCH FORMULA

Step 5   DMOZ.ORG Submission

Submit your web site to **dmoz.org**. This is a huge open directory that many smaller search engines go to get web sites for their database.

DMOZ is a web directory of Internet resources. The directory is hierarchically arranged by subject - from broad to specific. DMOZ is maintained by community editors who evaluate sites for inclusion in the directory. They are our experts, and all submissions are subject to editor evaluation.

https://dmoztools.net/docs/en/add.html

Chapter 11

BILLIONAIRE BUSINESS ADVICE

When They Talk, We Listen.

There is a link to YouTube videos created

by Evan Carmichael

Billionaire Business Advice

Bill Gates...

1. Have Energy

2. Have a Bad Influence

3. Work Hard

4. Create the Future

5. Enjoy what you do

6. Play Bridge

7. Ask for Advice

8. Pick Good People

9. Don't Procrastinate

10.   Have a sense of Humor

https://goo.gl/KE5CBT

Billionaire Business Advice

Mark Zuckerberg...

1. You get what you spend your time doing

2. Get Feedback

3. Make Mistakes

4. Only hire people who you would work for

5. Make a change in the world

6. Learn from the people around you

7. Build a really good team

8. Give the very best experience

9. Care the most about it

10.   Social bonds are critical

https://www.youtube.com/watch?v=HMpWXQpogqI&t=125s

Billionaire Business Advice

Oprah Winfrey...

1. Understand the next right move

2. Seize your Opportunity

3. Everyone makes mistakes

4. Work on yourself

5. Run the race as hard as you can

6. Believe

7. We are all seeking the same thing

8. Find your purpose

9. Stay grounded

10.   Relax its going to be okay

https://www.youtube.com/watch?v=7a8ncSBU-Eg

Michael Jordan...

1. Keep Working Hard

2. Ignite the Fire

3. Be Different

4. Fail Your Way to Success

5. Have High Expectations

6. Be Positive

7. Be who you were born to be

8. Have a vision

9. Stop Making EXCUSES

10.   Practice

https://www.youtube.com/watch?v=NidqtkXq9Yg&t=8s

Billionaire Business Advice

Holy Bible...

1. Have a vision:

"And the Lord answered me, and said, Write the vision, and make it plain upon tables, that he may run that readeth it" **Habakkuk 2:2**

2. Speak Life:

Death and life are in the power of the tongue: and they that love it shall eat the fruit thereof. **Proverbs 18:21**

3. Ask for what you want

Ye lust, and have not: ye kill, and desire to have, and cannot obtain: ye fight and war, yet ye have not, because ye ask not. **James 4:2**

4. Be willing to work for it

And he shall be like a tree planted by the rivers of water, that bringeth forth his fruit in his season; his leaf also shall not wither; and whatsoever he **doeth** shall prosper. **Psalm 1:3**

Holy Bible...

5. Accept Challenges

No discipline is fun while it lasts, but it seems painful at the time. Later, however, it yields the peaceful fruit of righteousness for those who have been trained by it. **Hebrews 12:11**

6. Give Back

Everyone should give whatever they have decided in their heart. They shouldn't give with hesitation or because of pressure. God loves a cheerful giver.

2 Corinthians 9:7

7. Tell the truth

But for the cowardly, the faithless, the vile, the murderers, those who commit sexual immorality, those who use drugs and cast spells, the idolaters and **all liars**—their share will be in the lake that burns with fire and sulfur. This is the second death."

Revelation 21:8

8. Reinvest your profits

In that case, you should have turned my money over to the bankers so that when I returned, you could give me what belonged to me with interest.

Matthew 25:27

9. Be thankful

"Give thanks to the Lord because he is good, because his faithful love lasts forever!"

Psalm 107:1

10.   Help others

The Samaritan went to him and bandaged his wounds, tending them with oil and wine. Then he placed the wounded man on his own donkey, took him to an inn, and took care of him.

Luke 10:34

Gold Medal Prayers: Brian Mahoney

https://goo.gl/GzeMAO

Please Leave a Review!

"It's better to be prepared for an opportunity and not have one, then to have an opportunity and not be prepared." Les Brown (You got to be hungry!)

I have had nice paying jobs. Safe and secure jobs. I worked for the government for over 23 years. But nothing compares to freedom.

Having your own business gives you more control over your life. When you have the proper knowledge you can increase your income and freedom based on the effort you are willing to put in.

This book gives you the knowledge to create opportunity.

I have enjoyed doing all the research and sharing my real world business experience in what I hope is a easy to understand, quick read, book.

Pursue your passion. Make every day a great day!

Thank you. Warm Regards,

Brian Mahoney

Link to leave a review.

Join Our VIP Mailing List And Get FREE Money Making Training Videos! Then Start Making Money Within 24 Hours!
Plus If You Join Our Mailing List You Can Get Revised And New Edition Versions Of Your Book Free!

And Notifications of other FREE Offers!

Just Hit/Type in the Link Below

https://mahoneyproducts.wixsite.com/win1

Zero Cost

Million Dollar

Internet Marketing

142 video series

Amazing Training Videos!

* YouTube Video Marketing

* Email Marketing

* Expert Copy writing

* Set up a Squeeze page

* Getting Massive Web Traffic

https://goo.gl/7t4XHY

Made in the USA
Monee, IL
08 January 2021